Creative
workshop

Hands-on learning, resources
and ideas for storytelling

Baltazar Boeuf

Creative writing workshop. Hands-on learning, resources, and ideas for storytelling

© Baltazar Boeuf, 2021.

All rights reserved.

Table of contents

FOREWORD	3
CHARACTERS AND PERSONALITY	5
CREATING THE PLOT	21
NARRATIVE UNIVERSES	29
BUILDING THE STRUCTURE	33
TRIGGERS	41
RECOMMENDED READINGS	47

FOREWORD

This is a practical book, with little theory and many exercises. Step by step you can shape and structure your narrative universe in order to tell credible and endearing stories.

Art is half technique and half mystery. The mystery of literature is about desires, impulses, needs, destiny and other inscrutable reasons. Inspiration can be encouraged but not taught, it is like faith, it exists or not. Technique, on the other hand, can be learned, taught, enriched and exercised.

Writing a story is a matter of practice, of reading a lot, and of knowing the tools and methods available. It does not matter if you are a beginner or if you have already written some books, this short manual will strengthen your weak points or help you discover new paths.

CHARACTERS AND PERSONALITY

They can convey antipathy, sympathy, fear, contempt, affection ... Every character must provoke some reaction in the reader. A character must be made of flesh, blood and spirit. Therefore, each appearance of them must show who they are, what are their doubts, fears, desires, as well as what they are capable of doing in certain circumstances.

During the plot development, characters will change. Through their learnings, journeys, victories, and defeats, they will be different from how the reader first met them. That is why it is very important to be very clear about who characters really are from the beginning. What do they think, what do they feel, what do they want?

To get to know your characters, I recommend you fill out a form with essential data, both physical and personality. Much of this information will not be known to the reader, but it will help you to give consistency to your characters. A thoroughly file will help you create more complete and vivid profiles. Try this model, from which you can add or delete data.

Character sheet

- Name
- Nickname (if any)
- Place of birth
- Place or places of residence
- Known activities
- Unknown activities
- Three ideas they have about life (what they want most, what they can't, what they hate, what they think life should be)
- Names and characteristics of three acquaintances or friends (if any)
- How does the character usually dress?
- How does he/she/it talk?
- What and where do they eat?
- A memory of their childhood
- Any peculiar physical details (limps, a missing eye, a bald head, long fingers, three ears, tattoos, etc.)?
- Where do they live?
- How do others perceive them?

Even a photograph of someone you think resembles your character or a drawing you have done yourself can help you give this profile more strength.

Remember that at first the reader will not know all this details about your character, and it is even possible that the character himself does not know everything about himself. But you, as the author, must know him -or her- very well, so that his -or her- evolution it be congruent. The characters in your novel or your stories will be your companions for several months, even years, so you must know them like no one else.

With the data on that sheet now write a brief description of that character, as you would like the reader's first impression to be. I don't mean copying every single piece of information from the sheet but arranging some of those elements in a situation that reveals something about the character's personality. Use, for example, a physical feature of the character, a recurring idea and the place where the character lives to assemble a situation in which we see the character in action.

In general, avoid being literal. For example, if your character smokes a lot, don't say "Ana smokes two cigarette packets every day," but show her in some situations lighting a cigarette or in desperation if she doesn't have one handy.

Once you know your character comes the second step: Knowing how he or she would react to certain situations.

Character conflicts

Characters should have internal and external conflicts. If they don't, consider whether they are relevant to your story.

Internal conflicts refer to the imbalance between desires, the feasibility of realizing them and the implicit morality between carrying them out.

So, ask your characters:

- What do they want or need?
- What can they do or what are they capable of doing?
- Should they act or not act? (To be or not to be)
- What are the consequences of their actions or inactions?

You'll find that your characters sometimes want something but can't or feel it's not the right thing to do; sometimes they have the power to modify the environment but don't want to; sometimes they know something would be the right thing to do (the good thing for the community in moral terms) but can't and don't want to do it.

Internal conflict is the dissonance between these three variables (desire, duty and power). If they were aligned, there would likely be no conflict at all and, therefore, no story worth telling.

- Now, based on the answers to the above questions, write your character's internal conflict. Remember that you already know something of his personality according to the information you wrote in the character's sheet and you know what he needs and what his strengths, weaknesses and ethical stance are. As mentioned above, it is likely that the character does not know himself so well. But you have no excuse, you must really know how far he will want or be able to go.

External conflict comprises all circumstances, problems or forces that prevent the fulfillment of the character's desires and duties. External conflicts can be social, political, economic, sentimental, religious, technological. In some cases the character will be able to maneuver very little, as is the case of destiny, however the resistance or letting go of each character is what will dictate the course of the story.

- Write an external conflict. For example:

   -a journalist who begins to investigate a criminal case and discovers that her relatives are involved,

   -the leader of a community who must confront the central power to prevent them from being dispossessed of their land,

-a just-married couple who get lost in the jungle,

-a prophet who predicts an imminent disaster but no one takes him seriously.

In all the proposed examples, remember that it is the profile of the character that gives relevance to the conflict. The journalist, the community leader or the prophet should not be hackneyed stereotypes, but should respond to the profile of the journalist, the leader or the prophet that you have previously constructed. Beyond the profession, duty or position of the character, it is their unique characteristics that will move the story.

It is important to know that the encounter between internal and external conflicts triggers the story.

The external conflict that triggers, or reveals, the internal conflict of the character is the engine of a good story. That's why I prefer to talk about characters before talking about plot or structure. Because it is the link between the characters' personalities and internal or external conflicts that will drive the plot.

The next step, then, is to relate the statement of the external conflict you wrote to the character's internal conflict:

- How much can he do?
- Can he do it without help?

- Does he prefer the general welfare or his own and those close to him?
- Does he really have a desire for things to change?
- What is he willing to sacrifice to get what he wants?

These kinds of answers will allow you to work on the development of the story, as you will be able to discover what the character's next steps will be and who his allies or adversaries will be.

Hero archetypes

Now you can outline the essential attributes of the characters in your story. If you have several characters but you are not yet clear what role they will play, you can classify them according to the archetypes of the hero.

Archetypes are atavistic models, patterns to behaviors, ideas, thoughts. Something very different are stereotypes, simplifications often based on prejudices. I make the distinction because I recommend avoiding the latter unless you do so deliberately to make a point.

A guide for you to know in which spectrum to place your characters are the archetypes of the hero studied by authors like Campbell and Vogler.

There are eight archetypes. They are not intended to pigeonhole your characters, but to help you place them according to the position they may adopt at different moments in the plot. Keep in mind that the same character can embody more than one of these archetypes in the same story.

1. The **hero**, or the **heroine**, refers to the main characters, who face the most relevant conflicts of the story through learning and experience. Heroes are imposed or self-imposed a mission and must fulfill it, not always successfully.

- Choose a protagonist from a novel you have read and write down his or her conflict, mission and learning.

2. The **mentor** is the guide or advisor, he prepares the hero, motivates him, gives him ideas or inputs. In classic stories it is usually the bearded old man full of experience, but surely you can think of a character who serves as a mentor and who does not fit that stereotype.

- Write a couple of situations where the protagonist is advised or helped by a mentor. What would this character be like? How could he or she help?

3. **Allies** are the hero's assistants, henchmen, collaborators or confidants. They know his secrets and almost always join his projects, complementing the skills and

thoughts of the protagonists. They are usually secondary or supporting characters, but in some cases, they are so relevant that they become true protagonists. For example, Sancho Panza or Doctor Watson not only accompany Don Quixote or Sherlock Holmes but are consubstantial to their adventures.

The allies are not blind followers of the hero, they can also question them or give them another perspective. In any case, they must encourage them to move forward.

- Make a list of several allied characters from novels you have read and write what the story would have been like without them. Would it really be the same story?

4. **Herald** is the messenger. They can collaborate with the heroes, they can oppose them or they can also be neutral. They are the ones who communicate a prophecy, a warning or information unknown to the protagonist. And although they are human beings or incarnations of human beings, they can also be spirits, animals, signs of nature or technological gadgets.

- In the story you would like to write, who could play this role: a blind seer, a tarot-reading witch, a gossipy janitor or a teenage hacker who can foresee what is going to happen?

In addition to the protagonists and their allies, there are characters who play a role for or against the hero as he progresses along his path. Their goals or alliances are not always clear and this ambiguity makes the story richer.

5. The **trickster** is the ironic, humorous, sometimes deceitful or cruel character that gives a note of black and crude humor to the narrative. They can be the character's ally, be on the side of the opponents or be on their own. They usually arouse a lot of contempt or empathy, but they are not indifferent to the reader.

6. The **shapeshifter** is the one who plays both sides, a chameleon-like character. Neither the reader nor the other characters are clear about his intentions or his objective. Sometimes he seems to collaborate with the protagonist to later reveal his true intentions. Or the opposite: he gets in his way because he was trying to help him but in his own way.

- In the context of the story you want to write, determine two characters who meet the archetype of the trickster and the shapeshifter. Describe them briefly and then introduce them in the story. Remember that the character sheet applies not only to the main characters but also to all the characters in your story.

7. The **guardian** is the oracle that tests the hero's worth. He protects the portals that block his way. He can be a character of

physical or intellectual strength: the effigy with its riddles or the three-headed dog guarding the entrance to the underworld. In a more contemporary and prosaic context, the guardian can be a defiant friend, a vigilant chaperone, an overprotective parent or a hacker guarding access to critical information.

- Think of a guardian type for your story. Remember that it can be something more modern and innovative, like an autonomous computer program, or the heavily guarded gates of a skyscraper, for example. What other ideas can you come up with?

8. Lastly (or first, since it usually appears as a trigger for the story) is the archetype of the **shadow.** We associate it with the idea of antagonist, opponent or enemy. In good stories this character should have the same preponderance as the protagonist. He is not just someone to defeat, but someone with whom the reader can empathize and understand to a certain extent.

Keep in mind that the idea of absolute evil can be a bit old-fashioned. The most memorable shadow characters are the ones that resemble the hero, even if it's in twisted mirror form. While all characters should be well constructed, it is especially the shadow that you need to pay more attention to, as it always runs the risk of resolving them into predictable stereotypes. I recommend that when you take the first steps in your story, think of the shadow as your hero, and vice versa.

- Set aside the prototypes and write a brief profile of a character who could be the shadow in your story. What drives him or her? Why should your reader want to listen to the shadow's arguments? Is he or she as right as the hero?

In short, each has a narrative function:

- Serve or sacrifice
- Guide
- Accompany
- Warn and challenge
- Disturb
- Question and deceive
- Destroy

Remember that these eight archetypes are not laws, they are guides to set the intentions and purposes of your characters. Above all, I invite you to mix these archetypes and turn them around to create original characters and situations.

Read the sentences and write a situation that fits the proposed archetypes:

- A herald who is always wrong in his predictions.

- A lazy hero who is forced to be a one.
- A heroine who becomes a shadow or vice versa.
- A heroine with no allies.
- A guardian who accepts bribes.
- A foolish and innocent shadow.

Come up with other subverted archetypes and write them down. Maybe one of them will be the germ of a new story to tell.

Personality types

There are alternative or complementary ways to deepen your characters, so that their actions and thoughts would be coherent and credible.

Have you heard about personality tests? Many of them are available on the Internet and, although they will not give us an exact profile -as a qualified expert would do- they can give us clues as to whether the personality of our characters corresponds to the characteristics we think they have.

- Type in your browser "online personality test" and fill out several of them by answering the questions as if you were in the skin of each of your characters.

Answering them is only a guide for you as the author, consider that these tests are based on different parameters and do not offer clinical results but approximations. Among them, the Myers-Briggs test of the 16 personality types can give you an idea of what characteristics predominate in your characters according to their ideas or behaviors in certain situations. Although you should not take the results literally, it is certainly a useful guide.

Another tip to give more depth and verisimilitude to your character is to ask questions to other characters about the one you are building.

- How do they see him or her?
- What do they know and what do they ignore?
- What do they think of their actions?

Obviously, the answers must be different and in some cases contradictory. So, it is in real life; even when it comes to recognized personalities there are opposing positions. Remember also that not all the characters in your story know the same about each other, so their perspective is biased. The important thing is that for you as the author (and consequently for the reader) each character is consistent with himself beyond the sympathy or antipathy he arouses in others.

- Test your characters by thinking about how they would react to different situations. For example, what would they do or think if...

... discovered she has three months to live.

.... discovered he was adopted.

.... finds a suitcase full of money in front of an abandoned house.

... in her place of work, she is forced to support a political cause with which she disagrees.

... her two children drown at the same time and he can only help one of them.

You can come up with exaggerated situations that have nothing to do with the tone of your novel because the idea is to get to know your character better, even in other scenarios. It is said that we human beings reveal our true personality in extreme situations.

If you've gotten this far, you already know your characters well enough to introduce them to the reader.

- Write the first lines in which the reader of your story will meet your character. In what situation will you introduce him or her? What physical or psychological aspects will you show first? What will your character say or think?

Take these lines as the ideal of that first impression you would like to give.

Remember: you can create common characters in not so common situations, or you can also create extravagant characters in common situations. Either path, or a mix of both, will serve you to create memorable characters.

CREATING THE PLOT

At this point you should have your characters already well outlined. Now you can insert them, place them and arrange them on the story canvas.

You probably thought of the plot first before the characters. This is perfectly normal. The advantage of doing it the other way around is that at this point the characters in your book (at least most of them) are now living, self-contained entities, and therefore the plot will be more believable.

In my experience as a writing teacher, it is recurrent to find that many trainees conceive a fabulous plot but fail to sustain it because their characters are simple and cardboard. Hence my insistence that it is the characters (their attitude toward the adversity) that produce the plot.

The plot is the set of events that support the storyline. While the **storyline** briefly answers "What is the story about?", the **plot** is how events occur, how they are linked together, and how they are resolved.

One example to state the storyline might be as follows: *After more than a decade away from her hometown, retired detective Johanna Storm returns to care for her father dying of a sudden terminal illness. She is reluctantly asked to help solve a criminal case. Only she manages to tie up the loose ends and, in piecing them together, discovers that her entire family background, including her father, is implicated in the crimes.*

You could give a little more information, although you probably won't know what the story will lead to after a certain point. The important thing is to know how it starts and when the tension begins.

- In no more than seven lines write the storyline of the story you want to tell. Here you should consider the internal and external conflicts that the main characters will face.

Now the task is to unravel the how. In the how lies the essence of your story.

It is not always possible to be clear about the whole plot, it usually emerges as you write. I am in favor of not knowing everything that is going to happen in a story because part of the adventure of writing is to discover as you write.

To outline the plot you need more space, since you must state (for your use as narrator) which voices will tell the story, when the events occur, which characters perform the main actions and which characters support them, how the events are linked, why some events occur and why others don't. We can say that the plot is a story that is a story, but it is not a plot. We can say that the plot is a storyline developed in detail.

The first step in developing the plot is to decide where to start telling the story:

Ab ovo (from the beginning):

    For example: the founding of a city or the life of a character from the moment of his or her birth.

In media res (from the middle of the events).

    For example: A fugitive tells the story of how he was unjustly imprisoned while still escaping.

In extremis (from the end):

    For example: An old woman on a lonely island begins to write her memoirs beginning from the most recent events to the most distant ones.

Regardless of where you start to tell the story, you can use resources such as flashbacks or flashforwards to refer to earlier or later moments of the story.

For example: McCall, Idaho, *2021, detective Johanna Storm suffers a traumatic accident that makes her ask for her definitive dismissal from the Homicide Department. Despite her multiple lovers, she leads a solitary and reserved life. She is moderately reputed for having solved important cases, but there are no major obstacles when she asks for her discharge. Weeks after her official retirement, she receives a call from her hometown, Villa Z., informing her that her father has a few months to live. Although it is a trip she would not have wanted to make, she says goodbye to her confidant and best friend, Louis Wallace, and sets out on the long journey to those mountains she had not seen for two decades. The town has changed a lot, many constructions and new streets; she feels lost and finds it difficult to locate the address of the house where she used to live. She is helped by a young woman named Piera who despite of...* And so on...

Based on this example, try to write in a couple of pages the whole development of your future plot. You must span at least up to the point where you considered it in the storyline.

In this example I mentioned four characters (the detective, her father, her male friend and the young woman who guides her when arrives to town). In this plot fragment we assume that the secondary characters have a vital purpose in relation to the main character's conflict: they will support her, hinder her path, betray her, and so on.

The secondary characters also have a story of their own in parallel to the main story. The development of their stories in the novel constitutes the secondary plots or **subplots**. They advance as the main plot progresses, and the actions of the characters in their own stories directly or indirectly affect the main plot.

Let's go back to the eight hero archetypes seen above. Imagine that one of your characters plays the role of female mentor. She must have her own story and the help or guidance she gives to the main character must be consistent with her own story.

Not every single character must have a subplot developed, but at least three or four of the relevant characters must. The subplot also gives coherence to why these secondary characters behave in this or that way.

The plot will be your guide to develop the structure of your book, as we will see later. I recommend that from the plot you imagine what will be that first scene or sentence that you want to present to the reader.

- Read the following beginnings. You may be familiar with these books and already know what they are about.

'It is a truth universally acknowledged, that a single man in possession of a good fortune, must be in want of a wife'.

Pride and Prejudice, Jane Austen

'When Gregory Samsa awoke one morning after a restless sleep, he found himself on his bed transformed into a monstrous insect'.

The metamorphosis, Franz Kafka

> *'He was an old man who fished alone in a skiff in the Gulf Stream and he had gone eighty-four days now without taking a fish'.*
>
> *The Old Man and the Sea*, Ernest Hemingway
>
> *On the day they were going to kill him, Santiago Nasar got up at 5:30 in the morning to wait for the ship in which the bishop was coming on.*
>
> *Chronicle of a Death Foretold*, Gabriel García Márquez

What do you think of these beginnings? Would you like the beginning of your story to be similar?

Don't be afraid to get straight to the point and tell the reader what the story is about from the first lines. Thus they'll want to move forward on to the next lines.

At this point you already know your main characters, their internal and external conflicts, and the plot of the story you will write.

What follows next is to establish what their character's primary and secondary goals are.

The characters must move forward little by little, overcoming different obstacles, sometimes going backwards and sometimes choosing another path. All these obstacles and bumps to overcome in order to achieve the main objective are the secondary objectives. These can be: getting permission from an authority, passing through a town to retrieve documents, get an interview, rescue a scientist who has important information, getting a weapon, collecting clues, etc.

- Based on the plot and the characteristics of your main characters, write down a list of secondary objectives that lead to the fulfillment of the main objective. Then, next to that list of objectives write the obstacles for each one.

Overcoming or defeating each of these obstacles is what allows the plot to advance. Between each advance, new characters and unexpected conflicts can be introduced.

These unexpected conflicts make the plot take unexpected turns, surprising the reader but also (and above all) the characters. This is what is known as plot twists: a call that makes the protagonist return to his homeland, the discovery of a truth or a treasure map, the confessed criminal who turns out to be innocent, the return of someone who was thought dead, the recovery of memory about transcendental events, a spurious conspiracy that ends with the execution of the alleged subversives, the good Samaritan who reveals himself to be a traitor, the character who discovers that he was always dead and that the dead ones were actually the living, etc.

These twists and turns can shift the story in a different direction than the reader expects. A good story should have a few twists and turns to keep the reader hooked, but don't use them too much or the plot will be diluted, and the reader will get tired of too many surprises. There is no magic number for plot twists, but I recommend no more than five.

NARRATIVE UNIVERSES

The characters and the development of the adventures take place in specific locations. Whether they are imagined or real, you must construct them in such a way that the reader can feel how your characters feel, move and interact with the environment.

As you create your characters and develop the plot, you will be introduced to a variety of settings, many of which should have as much life and "personality" as the characters themselves. Think about the books you love and try to remember the places where they take place. If you can bring them back to life and feel like you're there, it's because the author worked those landscapes and places very well.

- Identify the settings of your story: a city, a village, the jungle, the fjords? What are the recurring places: a hut, a cafeteria, a prison, inside a computer program? In all cases you must specify the characteristics of these places. Whether they are fictional or real, you must be very clear about what they are like and what it feels like to be there.

The narrative universe of the story is linked to the time in which it happens. Knowing the time in which you develop your story goes beyond a scenography question, you must also take into account what that time is like and what are the social values that predominate.

Places determine (and are determined by) social relations, culture, communications, history, economy. Depending on space and time, you must make the environment clear through questions such as the following: How do the characters dress? What do they eat, at what time? What kind of jobs do they do for a living? How do they spend their time? How do they travel from one place to another? What are the morals of the time on certain issues (death penalty, euthanasia, slavery, family relationships...?

These are questions that seem obvious when you look at them from today's eye, but remember that every universe changes over time and with geographic location.

- Choose two of the books you like the most and write in a paragraph what the predominant narrative universe is like. Leave aside the plot and focus on telling what that space is like.

Narrative universes are closely related to the psychological sensation they transmit. An oppressive, labyrinthine enclosure with gray walls and no windows conveys something very different from a luminous open space with green meadows, streams and wild animals. In each case your characters will feel very differently.

- Describe in ten to twelve lines a place that conveys each of the following feelings:

  Wealth

  Power

  Desolation

  Loneliness

  Hope

  Anxiety

Keep in mind that a landscape has not only shape and dimensions, but also colors, sounds and smells.

A good source of inspiration is to look for images or select a color palette through which you can imagine places. You can also dedicate a soundtrack to that place to set the mood and be in tune with a particular state of mind when describing that place or setting a scene in it.

You can also make sheets for relevant places that will appear in your story. For example:

- Name of the place
- Extension
- Location
- Antiquity

- Period in which the history takes place
- Remarkable buildings
- Climate
- Recurring locations (someone's room, the police station, a restaurant, a basement*)
- Adjacent spaces (another city, other planets, another room)
- How do the characters move in the spaces (do they walk, do they take the subway, do they take ships, do they communicate via the internet but without moving?
- How do the people who live there feed themselves?
- How do the characters socialize in that space?
- What does the place smell like, what is the music or colors that might identify it?

*You can also dedicate a sheet to these smaller spaces. It all depends on the relevance and frequency of appearance.

BUILDING THE STRUCTURE

After knowing your characters, the possible plot and the universe in which the story takes place, you must now think about the structure you want to give to your book.

Regardless of whether it is linear, circular or disordered and fragmented, the important thing is to be clear about what you prefer to tell first and what to leave in suspense for later. In many cases the suspense is not only for the reader, but many authors do also not know what is going to happen.

It is valid if you decide to tell the story from the beginning, from the middle or from the end. The order is a work of final carpentry that you can modify at your discretion.

The clearer you are about the path your characters should take, the easier it will be to arrange of an alternative order or use resources such as flashbacks or flashforwards mentioned in the plot chapter.

Following the classic hero's journey, write the situations that would be part of your story according to the following scheme:

- The hero's world before he feels or is driven to act. The zero point or genesis of the story.
- The crisis that pushes him to act or disrupts his world.
- The reluctant or fearful attitude of the protagonist to step out of his comfort zone.
- The mentor's revelation or advice to push him to act. The words of the herald who will tell him what will happen if he does not act.
- The protagonist's first action to face the conflict.
- His first missteps and interactions with his allies and enemies.
- His deep immersion in the conflict. Discovery that the conflict was greater than he had estimated.
- The protagonist's suffering, partial defeats and partial victories.
- The reward or attainment of achievements and recognition.
- The return to the place of origin of the conflict, to his life as it was before, or to his new life.
- The rebirth (physical or emotional).
- The exhibition of the achievement.

You may not yet know what to fill in each part, since you are one of those writers who prefer to discover. It may also happen that you feel that there are certain parts that would have no place in your story (for example, the reward or the rebirth).

In fact, I invite you to flip some of these parameters to achieve greater originality in your story.

For example, in your character's journey you can have a series of initial victories and from then on it's all defeats. Or, as we have discussed in character archetypes, your hero may be someone who not only rejects the first call but refuses to act throughout the story and events happen in spite of him.

The important thing is that the characters undergo a change, a learning or even an unlearning.

Each of these sections (genesis, revelation, suffering, reward, return, etc.) is composed of scenes. A **scene** is the minimal narrative unit that takes place in the same place, at the same time and with the same characters.

The ordered list of key moments or scenes (depending on how exhaustive you want to be beforehand) is what is known as a **step outline**.

A step outline like the following chart can help you organize the plot of your story.

Chapter*	Scene*	Scene purpose	What happens?	Characters involved	Place	Time

*I recommend that you give the chapters and scenes not only a number but also a name to guide you. For example:

> Chapter II
>
> (Discovery of patient zero).
>
>> Scene 5
>>
>>> (Dr. Marian is fired from the lab when it is confirmed that she tampered with the samples).

There can be as many scenes as your story needs. Each one should have a specific function, so ask yourself if your scene serves any of the following purposes:

- Introduces or complicates a conflict.
- Introduces a character.
- Reveals information that moves the story forward or changes its course.
- Achieves a partial resolution of a conflict or spoils a previous breakthrough.
- Shows what a character thinks of the conflict or how the conflict changes the character.
- Connects two characters for the first time, strengthens or damages their relationship.
- Shows a relevant scenario.

These objectives will help you to validate whether your scene contributes to the story and also to come up with situations that will allow the plot to progress.

Keep in mind that a story is not one hundred percent narration. It may contain **thoughts of the narrating voice**, comments on the story and about life. These passages -where not much is happening in terms of action- give the story support and can serve as a transition from one scene to another. For example, the narrator (whether in first or third person) can reflect on ideas such as love, war, exile, crime, loneliness. This contribution not only occurs in philosophical terms but can also provide information, comments or analysis of a scientific, technological, financial, etc.

The important thing is that the scenes are linked to the scenes that precede and follow them so that they are not a set of isolated events.

A chapter is usually made up of several scenes. Each scene is the notch of a clockwork mechanism that can go as fast as the speed you want to give to your story. For example, the revelation of an important secret can happen in a single scene. But if the rhythm of your story advances at a slow pace, you can gradually spread the revelation over several scenes. Like this:

- the heroine meets a herald who promises to tell him something important,
- the herald performs an action to gain the heroine's trust,
- the herald and the heroine have differences that separate them,
- the two come into contact again,
- they regain trust,
- the herald entrusts the heroine with the prophecy.

Another complementary way to order the events of the story is to work with **timelines**. It is similar to a step outline, but its main purpose is to ensure that there are no jumps, bumps or temporal inconsistencies in the plot, as well as to order the events. Regardless of the order in which your plot unfolds, drawing a timeline is important so that there is coherence between what you are telling.

If you have decided to write a **polyphonic** narrative in which many characters tell a fragment of the story, the timelines will help you to achieve coherence and the globality of the story.

In the case of novels with many voices, or with chapters based on documents, you can design your own structure. The important thing is that you distribute the information and that each section leads first to the climax and then to the resolution.

In such a story type you can insert fragments of each of these documents to alternate several voices according to the format:

- **Narrator A** (interviews) Chapters 1, 7, 13
- **Narrator B** (letters) Chapters 2, 8, 14
- **Narrator C** (a logbook or personal diary) Chapters 3, 9, 15
- **Narrator D** (police or forensic reports) Chapters 4, 10, 16
- **Narrator E** (apocryphal document or newspaper articles) Chapters 5, 11, 17
- **Narrator F** (the characters who narrate in the first person tell their experience in relation to the events) Chapters 6, 12, 18...

In this and all the model structures, I reiterate the recommendation that you should write very descriptive titles or names for the scenes, chapters or sections so that you have a guide of what to tell in each one of them. It doesn't matter if at the end you decide to change those titles for more suggestive ones or simply not to use titles, but only numbers or separators.

TRIGGERS

Ideas for inspiration

As we commented in the prologue, this is a practical and brief book to use when you feel stuck or when you don't know where to start. It is a guide, one of many, but quite summarized and precise. I am not a fan of eternal courses, or endless or very rigorous and schematic manuals. Take all these elements as a lighthouse but skip them as many times as you want.

My final recommendation is that you should not forget that as a writer you are also (and above all) a reader. I invite you to apply the resources practiced in this manual to the books you like the most, regardless of the genre. Every time you read or reread, try to identify the personality and motivations of the characters, the role they play in the story, how they are presented, how places are described, how the story is paced, what are the twists and turns, and what is the structure the author decided to use.

If you're still feeling stuck, here are some triggers and tips that will help you to generate ideas or at least to exercise your imagination, your pen or your keyboard.

- Choose the beginning or a short excerpt from a fiction book and complete it in your own way. Here's a famous one.

"All blissful families are alike, but unhappy ones are each in their own way."

Anna Karenina, Lev Tolstoy.

- Select a story at random from the newspaper and write about those involved as if they were characters from a book. Don't just write about the actions they committed but speculate about who these people are, what their backgrounds are, their conflicts, their motivations.

- Select a painting or photograph that you like and write about it. What is happening there? If you could go inside that image, what would happen next?

- Imagine that someone wakes up in an abandoned warehouse. Write how he or she got there and how he or she would get out.

- Act out a scene you are writing. Read aloud the lines. Did you find the movements, postures, gestures and dialogues convincing, realistic, and coherent? Now rewrite it based on what you detected in that performance. You are scriptwriter, set designer and director of the play at the same time.

- Visit, preferably on foot, an unknown place near your neighborhood. Get out of your comfort zone. Write down what you discovered. Strive on a daily basis to discover the strange in the everyday.

- Start cultivating the habit of writing down your dreams as soon as you wake up.

- Even if you are not very sociable, seek to strike up a conversation with a stranger who seems interesting to you, or pay attention to conversations you may encounter along the way. Fill in the background and subsequent events of those dialogues.

- Take a classic story and write it in reverse, leaving the climax and surprising resolution at the beginning.

- Take the same classic tale and modify the role and personalities of the characters.

- Randomly open three literature books. With the first couple of sentences of each page write a new and coherent story.

- Choose words you like and write an innovative definition for each.

- Think of people you know by sight and write a story about their lives. Imagine they are keeping a secret and you are the one who begins to discover it.

- Locate a place and write a story from the perspective of an inanimate object (an office drinking fountain, a park bench, a traffic light on the street, a grocery cart).

- Imagine that a relevant object from the past was not invented (the wheel, vaccines, books) and write what the world would be like today without that object and all the implications derived from it.

- Write the possible dialogue between characters from different stories: Dr. Frankenstein with Sherlock Holmes. Don Quixote with Madame Bovary.

- Write the possible dialogue between real characters: Jorge Luis Borges with Napoleon. Frida Kahlo with Charles Darwin.

- Don't read only fiction. Read biographies, chronicles, essays, critical texts. From those readings write down ideas or scenarios that could be the germ of a story.

- Take an in-person or online creative writing workshop to share your progress and solve specific doubts.

Whether you have purchased the digital or print edition of this book, I encourage you to complete all the exercises at least three times. You will see how your ideas change and evolve.

I would greatly appreciate it if you would leave me a review or a few stars on the purchase rating page.

***

I did an experiment: I took all the suggestions I wrote for this manual and turned them around. The result was a novel of absurd humor titled **The Half Room**. If you would like to read it, here is the link.

Recommended readings

Calvino, Italo. *Why Read the Classics?* Vintage, 2001.

Campbell, Joseph. *The Hero with a Thousand Faces*. New World Library, 2008.

King, Stephen. *On Writing: A Memoir of the Craft*. Pocket Books, 2002.

Vogler, Christopher. *The Writer's Journey: Mythic Structure for Writers*. Michael Wiese Productions, 2007.

About the author

Baltazar Boeuf (Valletta, 1971). Writer, translator, and photocopier guy. Author of The Half Room, *The Rebel Right*, *New Philosophy of Pain* and *Summer Camp*. Founding member of Babel Project. He has lived in the cities of Mérida, Caracas, Madrid, Mexico City, Portland, Los Angeles and Coronel Pringles.